SIX COUNTRY DANCES
FOR VIOLIN & PIANO
RICHARD RODNEY BENNETT

NOVELLO

CONTENTS

Cover design: Fresh Lemon
Music setting: Robin Hagues
Photograph of Richard Rodney Bennett by Katie van Dyck

NOV950600
ISBN 1-84449-166-8

© Copyright 2003 Novello & Company Ltd.
Published in Great Britain by Novello Publishing Limited.

Head office
8/9 Frith Street, London W1D 3JB, England
Tel: +44 (0)20 7434 0066
Fax: +44 (0)20 7287 6329

Sales and hire
Music Sales Limited,
Newmarket Road, Bury St Edmunds, Suffolk IP33 3YB, England
Tel: +44 (0)1284 702600
Fax: +44 (0)1284 768301

www.chesternovello.com
e-mail: music@musicsales.co.uk

to Charles Hart
with affection and gratitude

SIX COUNTRY DANCES

1. All in a garden green

Richard Rodney Bennett

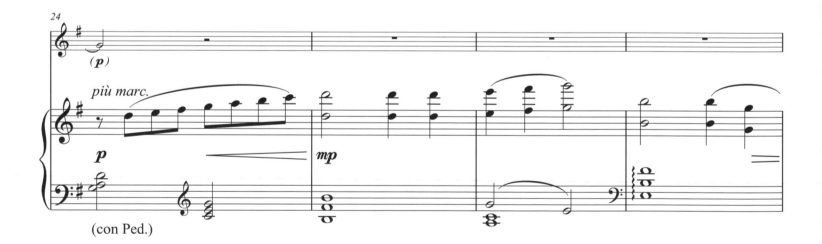

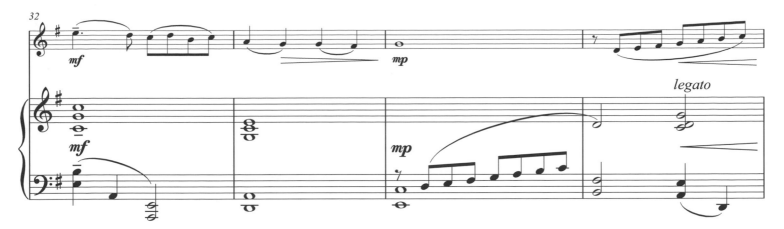

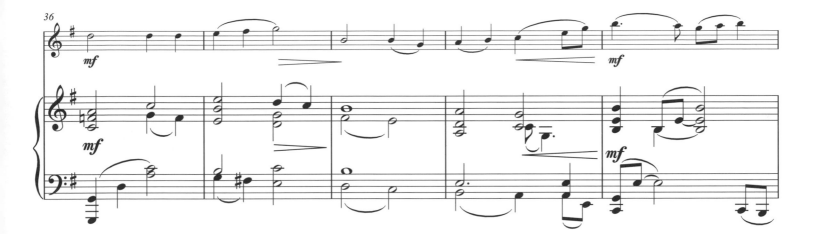

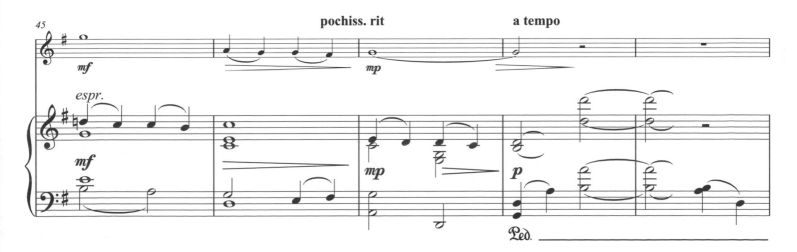

4

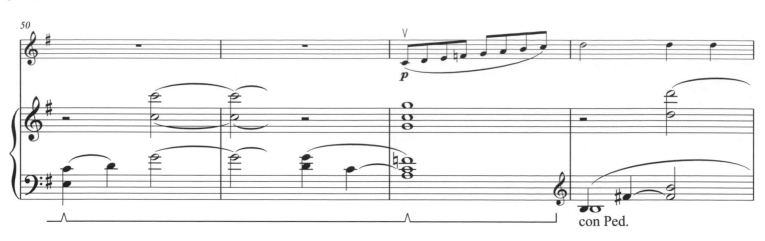

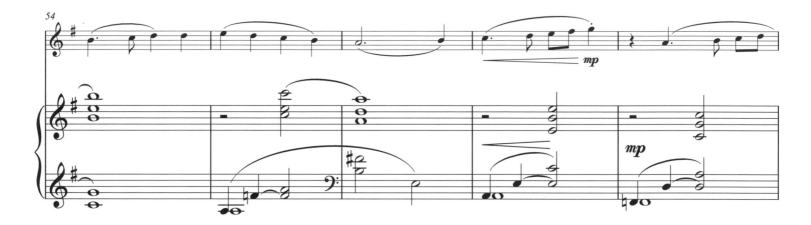

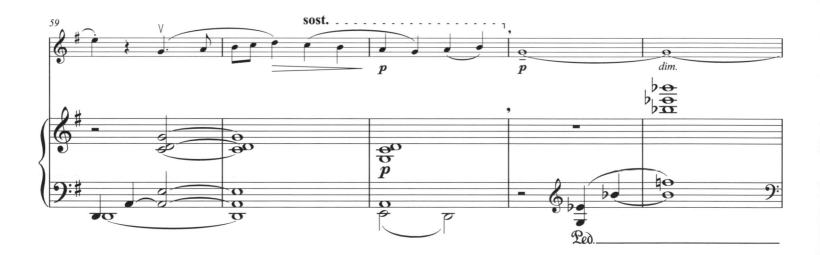

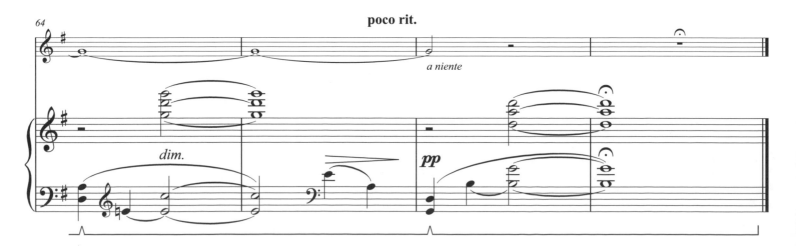

2. Buskin

6

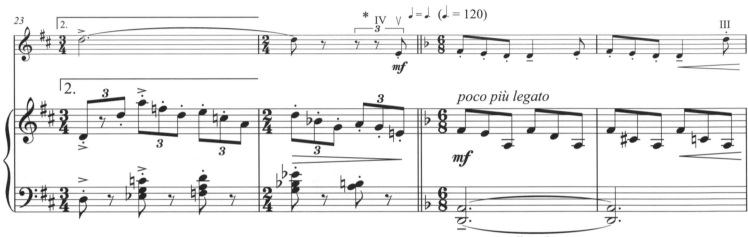

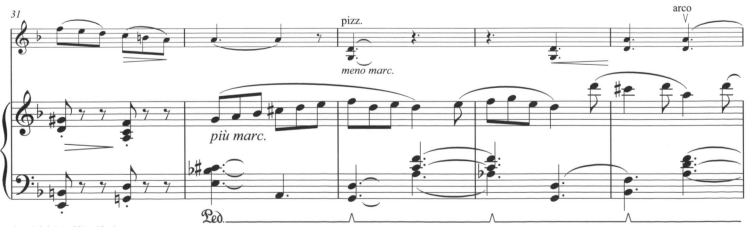

* 'Old Noll's Jig'

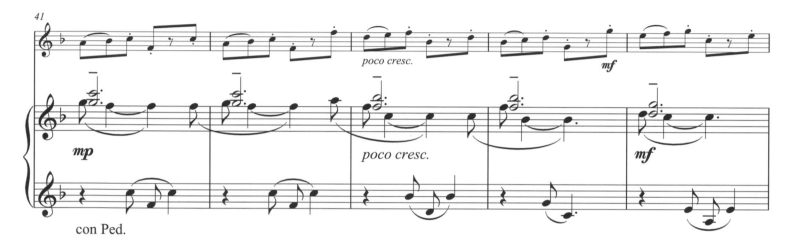

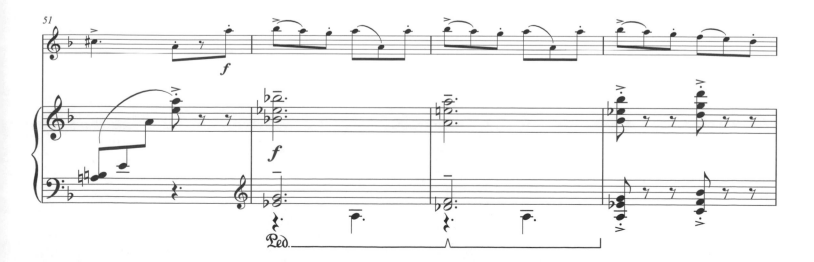

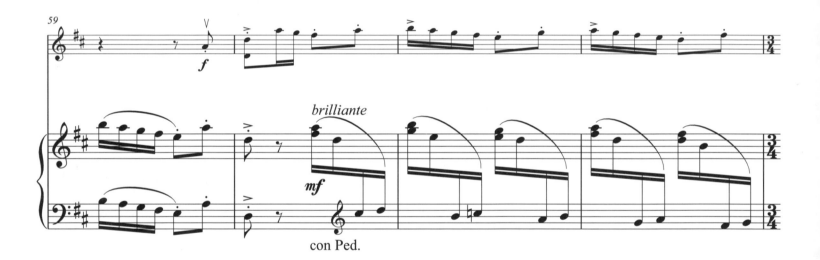

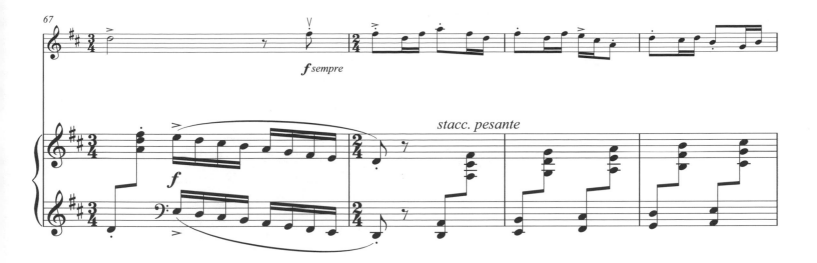

3. The Ladies' Misfortune

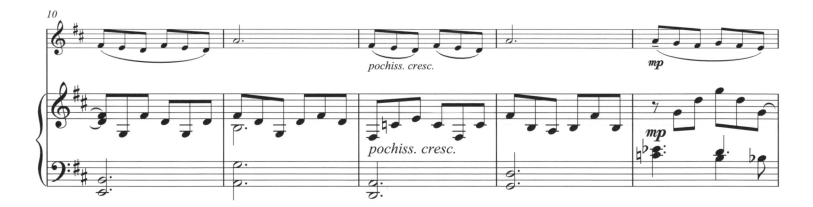

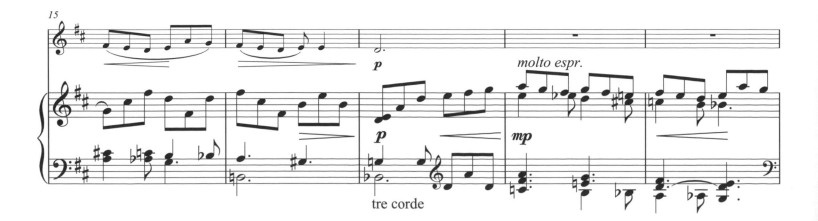

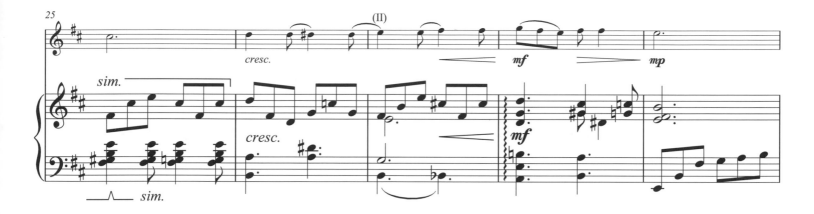

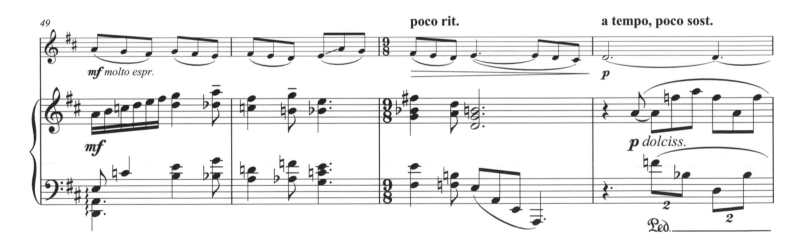

SIXCOUNTRYDANCES
FOR VIOLIN & PIANO
RICHARD RODNEY BENNETT

NOVELLO

CONTENTS

Cover design: Fresh Lemon
Music setting: Robin Hagues
Photograph of Richard Rodney Bennett by Katie van Dyck

NOV950600
ISBN 1-84449-166-8

Head office
8/9 Frith Street, London W1D 3JB, England
Tel: +44 (0)20 7434 0066
Fax: +44 (0)20 7287 6329

Sales and hire
Music Sales Limited,
Newmarket Road, Bury St Edmunds, Suffolk IP33 3YB, England
Tel: +44 (0)1284 702600
Fax: +44 (0)1284 768301

www.chesternovello.com
e-mail: music@musicsales.co.uk

Violin

to Charles Hart
with affection and gratitude

SIX COUNTRY DANCES

1. All in a garden green

Richard Rodney Bennett

Violin

52

57

62

2. Buskin

Vivo e ritmico (♩ = 120)

7

12

18

23

28

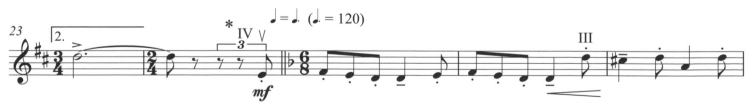

* 'Old Noll's Jig'

Violin

3. The Ladies' Misfortune

4. Enfield Common

* pluck with 2 fingers

5. Chelsea Reach

Blank Page

6. The Czar of Muscovy

Aug. 12th, 2000
New York City

4. Enfield Common

* pluck with 2 fingers

5. Chelsea Reach

Dolce espressivo (♩. = 40)

con Ped.
(tre corde)

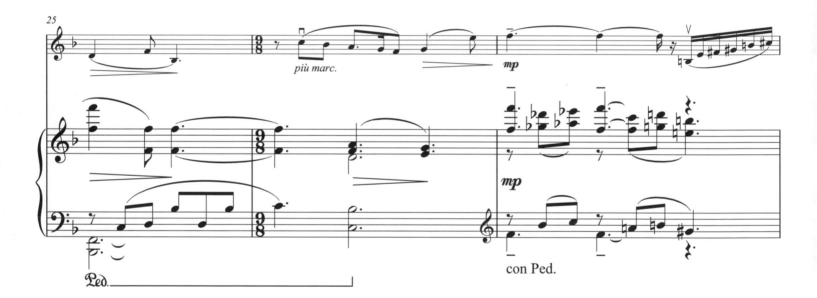

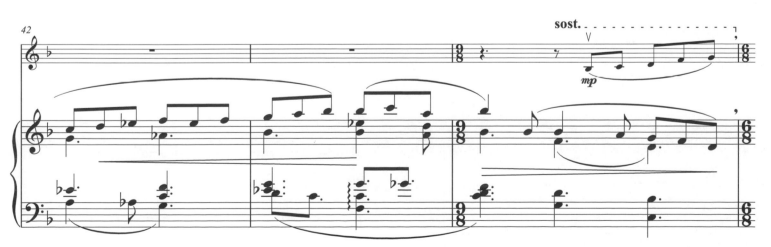

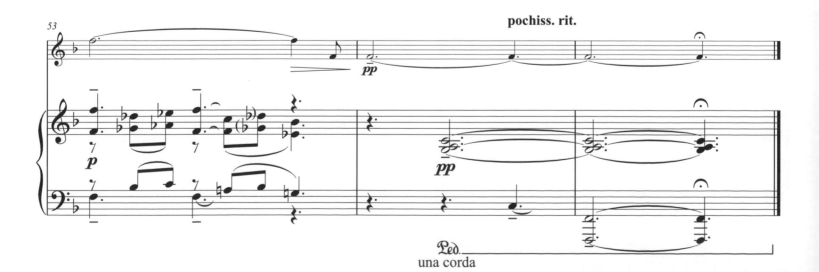

6. The Czar of Muscovy

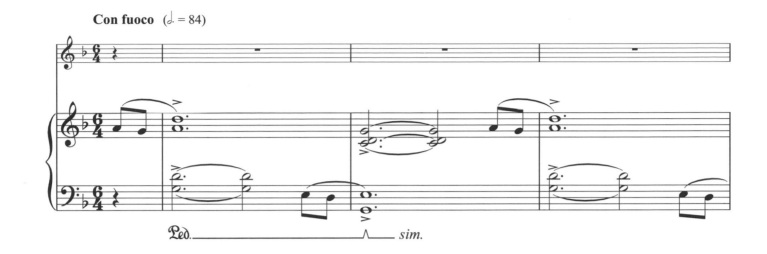

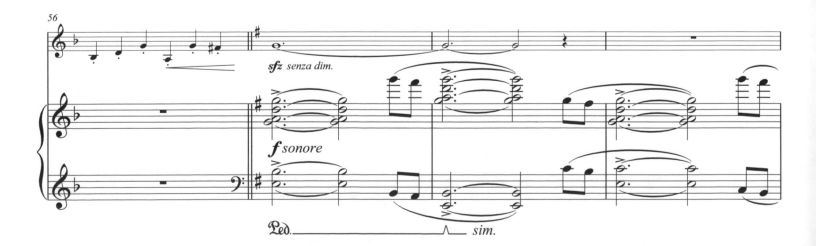

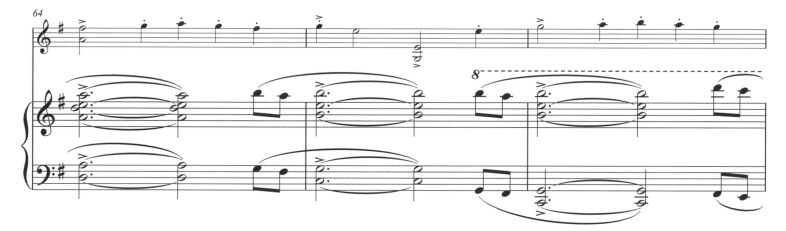

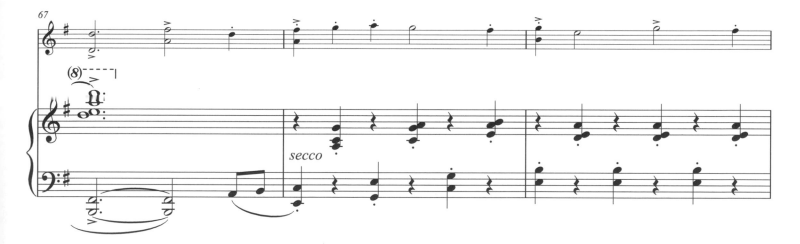

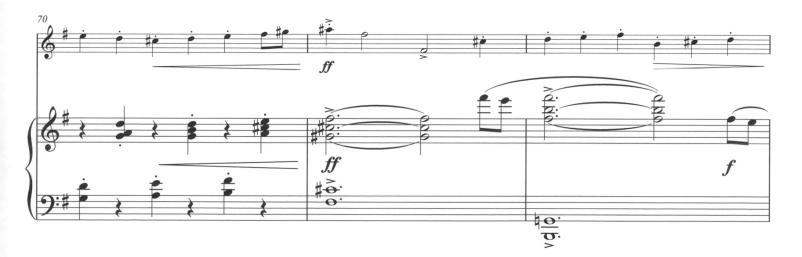

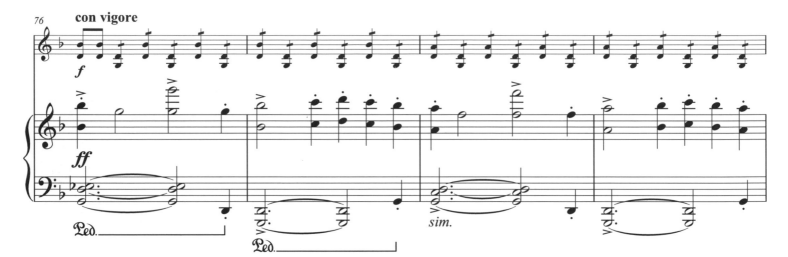

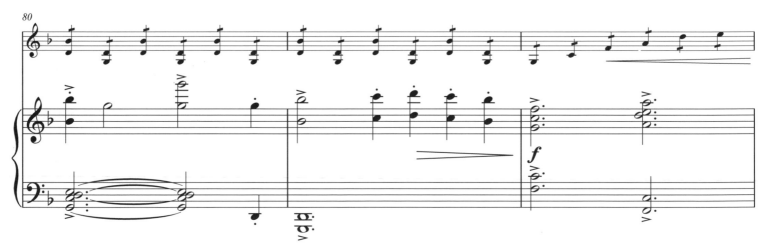

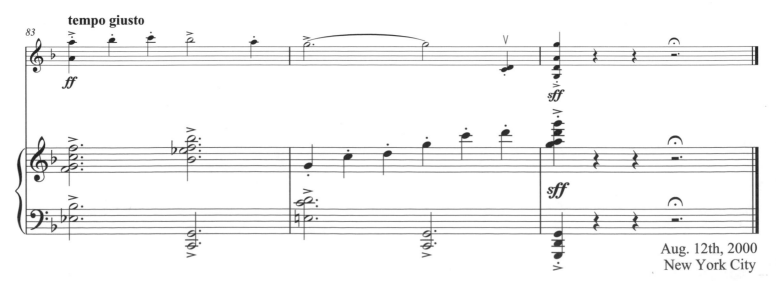

Aug. 12th, 2000
New York City